My First Book about Rhinoceroses

Amazing Animal Books

Children's Picture Books

By Molly Davidson

Mendon Cottage Books

JD-Biz Publishing

Read More Amazing Animal Books

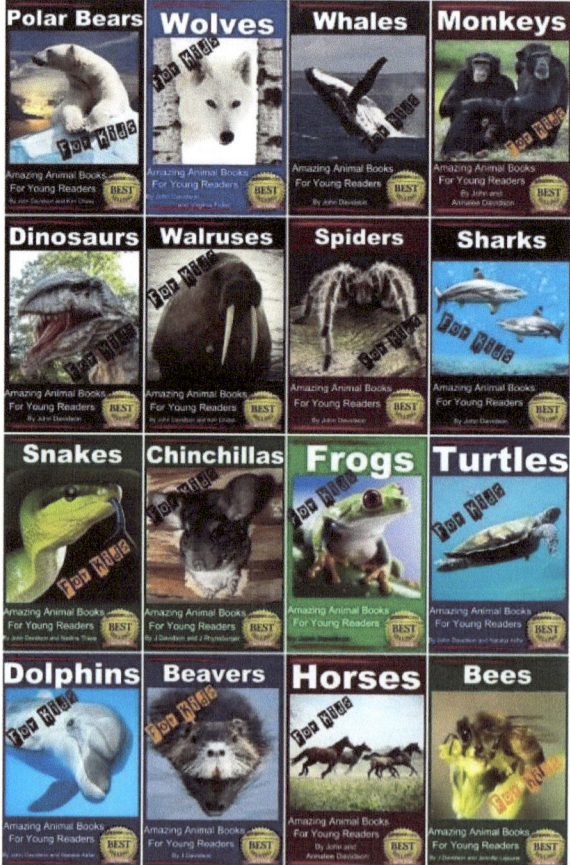

Download Free Books!

http://MendonCottageBooks.com

Table of Contents

Introduction

Rhinos are one of the major attractions at most zoos and wildlife preserves.

In Greek, the word rhinoceros means nose horn.

There are species of rhino that live in Asia and Africa; the African rhinos are the biggest.

Many rhinos will let an oxpecker ride on their back, in return the bird will watch for danger and make a loud sounding special alarm, if there is harm.

Rhinoceroses like to live by themselves.

They have really bad eyesight, so if you see when charging into a tree or ant hill, it's most likely because they cannot see very well.

About Rhinoceroses

Rhinos have been around since dinosaur time, about 23 million years.

A rhino's habitat can be the Savanna Desert, a thick forest, or a tropical area.

They eat mostly plants, grasses, and tree leaves.

They have a thick hide which helps them handle dry conditions.

A rhino's brain is small for their huge body size.

They use their horns to battle for the girl rhinos and territories, but also as self-defense against predators such as, tigers, lions, and hyenas.

Their horns are a great help when breaking branches or digging up roots to find food.

The lifespan of a wild rhinoceros is about 35 years.

What a Rhino Looks Like

Rhinos are usually grey, and can have one or two horns.

Their horns are made of keratin, not bone.

They do not have any hair, just tough, thick, and wrinkled skin.

Their skin can be up to 1 1/2 inches thick, plus they have two layers of fat under that.

They stand about 6 feet tall and weigh between 3,000 - 8,000 pounds, which is the size of a truck!

Their feet have heavy hooves that help them walk through thick forests while crushing twigs and brush to leave a clear, wide trail behind them.

How Rhinos Act and Talk

Rhinoceroses like to be left alone, so they may become angry if they are bothered.

Sometimes you may see a rhino charging at nothing, this is because they may sense (they have very good hearing and smell) something is near, but they cannot see it.

In order to attack, they gallop at a speed of 30 mph after snorting with their heads lowered and ears laid down.

Rhinoceros talk using many sounds like snorts, grunts, squeaks, bellows, and growls.

Rhinos can sleep both standing and lying on ground.

When curious or interested about something, they will straighten up their ears.

Rhinos mark their territories using dung piles. They scrape their feet on their dung pile leaving a trail of scent which tells others they are there.

Threats to Rhinoceros

Adult rhinos don't have any natural predators except for humans.

Poachers kill rhinoceros for their horns; some people believe they have healing powers and can keep evil spirits away.

Rhino horns are sold mostly in Asia, and most of those are sold in the country of Vietnam.

Rhinoceros horns are made of keratin, the same substance that our hair and nails are made of.

If we could get people to believe grinding up finger nails would heal them just like a rhino's horn, we would be able to save the rhinoceros.

White Rhinoceros

White rhinoceros is also called the square lipped rhinoceros; live in the grassy plains of Africa.

Their square lips make it easier for them to graze on grass and grains.

They are not actually white, they are a grey color.

They drink water twice a day, but can go up to 3 or 4 days without water, if it is a dry season.

White rhinos are about 13 feet long.

They grow two horns on their nose, which grow to be about 3 feet long!

Boy white rhinoceroses live alone, but the girls will live in herds of up to 14.

Rhinos like to get muddy, it helps keep the sun off their skin, as well as bugs.

White rhinos can run up to 50 mph!

Black Rhinoceros

Black rhinoceros, also called the hook-lipped rhinoceros, live in eastern Africa including; South Africa, Zimbabwe, Kenya, Cameroon, Angola, Tanzania, and Namibia.

They are not black; they are a brown and grey color.

Black rhinos have a hook lip which helps them eat trees, leaves, and twigs.

They weigh 1,700 - 3,000 pounds, on average, and stand 4 - 6 feet tall.

Their two ears move in separate directions to help them hear danger, since they can't see very well.

Black rhinos like to fight, and charge at anything that may every possibly be a threat.

Almost half of all black rhinos die because of injuries from fighting.

Indian Rhinoceros

Indian rhinoceros live in India and Nepal.

They are the second largest rhino, behind the white rhino.

Indian rhinos only have one horn; and they have bumps on their shoulders and legs.

They only have hair on the top of their ears, end of their tails, and as eyelashes.

Indian rhinos like to live alone, but they do hangout at bathing areas, and sometimes have to cross through each others territories.

They are great swimmers and can run up to 55 mph.

An Indian rhinoceros eats grasses, fruits, leaves, branches of trees, and shrubs; also floating or underwater plants.

They spend most of the day in rivers, puddles, lakes, and ponds; this helps keep them cool.

Javan Rhinoceros

The Javan rhinoceros is almost extinct; they only live in Java, Indonesia.

Only boy Javan rhinos have one small horn, which is about 7 1/2 inches long.

They do not use their horns for fighting; they are used to clear paths through forests, and to get food down from the trees.

Javan rhinos have an armor looking skin like the Indian Rhinos, but they are smaller.

Sumatran Rhinoceros

The Sumatran rhinoceros is the smallest rhino; they weigh between 1,100 to 2,200 pounds.

They have two horns and stand about 3 1/2 to 4 1/2 feet tall.

Sumatran rhinoceros lives in cloud forests, swamps, highland and lowland rainforests.

Bruce 1ee © <u>Wikimedia Commons</u>

They move to higher ground up in the hills during the rainy winter season.

International Rhino Foundation © <u>Wikimedia Commons</u>

Sumatran rhinos eat about 110 pounds of food per day, which is roots, trees, leaves, and fruit.

Even though they have small horns, they are being killed for them at a fast rate.

Interesting Facts about the Rhinoceros

Many other animals are named after the rhino because they have horns on the front of their heads too, like the rhinoceros fish, rhinoceros beetle, rhinoceros rat snake, rhinoceros cockroach, rhinoceros iguana, rhinoceros chameleon, rhinoceros viper, and rhinoceros hornbill.

A Rhinoceros Fish

A group of rhinos is called a herd or a crash.

Rhino's horns keep growing through their whole life.

Tigers, lions, hyenas, Nile crocodiles, and leopards will try to eat rhinos, usually the babies.

World Rhino Day is celebrated on September 22nd each year.

Rhinoceros in different cultures

A Malaysian legend says that rhinoceros used to put out fire in forests in order to protect the habitats of other animals.

Ground up horns of rhinos had been used in the making of Chinese medicine for hundreds of years. This is why the rhino is at risk f becoming extinct.

In Yemen, handles of weapons, such as daggers, are made using horns.

Rhinoceros is used as a mascot for many logos by advertisers. They believe it shows they are tough and strong; Rhino Lining is one example.

Conclusion

We hope you have enjoyed learning lots of information about rhinos today.

Join our newsletter and receive

Our books are available at

1. Amazon.com

2. Barnes and Noble

3. Itunes

4. Kobo

5. Smashwords

6. Google Play Books

Download Free Books!

http://MendonCottageBooks.com

Publisher

JD-Biz Corp

P O Box 374

Mendon, Utah 84325

http://www.jd-biz.com/

www.ingramcontent.com/pod-product-compliance
Lightning Source LLC
Chambersburg PA
CBHW050837290526
45792CB00001B/435